Seven
Spiritual
Laws of
Success

D A V I D . C . C O O P E R

The Seven Spiritual Laws of Success

Library of Congress Catalog Control Number: 00-093371

ISBN 0-9668382-2

Cover photography by Dan McClure.
Cover design by Mark Johnson.

To Barbie,
my faithful partner in every
success I have enjoyed.

Daniel,
Congratulation's on
your graduation.
God has great
things in store for
you!
Pastor Cooper
Proverbs 3:5-6

WHAT IS SUCCESS?

Everyone wants to be successful. The question is, how do you measure success? Webster says that success is, "a favorable or desired outcome of something attempted; a prosperous or advantageous issue or the attainment of wealth, fame, and so forth."

I like Winston Churchill's definition better: *Success is going from one failure to another without losing your enthusiasm.*

A Gallup Poll conducted on 1500 prominent people, revealed five common traits of successful people — common sense, knowing one's field, self-reliance, general intelligence, and the ability to get things done.

Is that all there is to success? Jesus responds with a heart-penetrating question, "*What good will it be for a man if he gains the whole world, yet forfeits his soul?"* (Matthew 16:26). Obviously, there is more to success than meets the eye.

Emerson's reflections on success call for a deeper definition:

How do you measure success?

To laugh often and much;

To win the respect of intelligent people and the affection of children;

To earn the appreciation of honest critics and endure the betrayal of false friends;

To appreciate beauty;

To find the best in others;

To leave the world a bit better whether by a healthy child, a redeemed social condition, or a job well done;

To know even one other life has breathed easier because you lived — this is to have succeeded.

It has been said that if you aim at nothing you will probably hit it — *nothing!* So, let's work on a definition of success so we'll know what we're aiming at. My mother handed me this note when I was in college: *Success is...to be able to carry money without spending it; to bear an injustice without retaliating; to keep on the job until it is finished; to do one's duty even when no one is watching; to accept criticism without letting it defeat you.*

Success is more than *fame*. There are many famous people in the world who we would hardly call successful. I mean, Fidel Castro has fame. He is known around the world. But he's a ruthless dictator who has amassed great wealth while subjecting his people to poverty, suffering and a constant struggle to attain freedom. He's famous, but not successful.

Success is more than *fortune*. The world is filled with wealthy individuals who have never done anything to make the world a better place in which to live. Gangsters are wealthy. Drug dealers are wealthy. Rock stars who promote violence, gore and death are wealthy. Media moguls who have filled America with the worst of the printed page are wealthy. But are they successful? Hardly.

Success is more than *pleasure*. Hedonism is alive and well in America. The hedonist advocates, "Whatever feels good, do it!" King Solomon tried to find success in pleasure. He indulged every desire and impulse. But after all was said and done he wrote, *"I thought in my heart, 'Come now, I will test you with pleasure to find out what is good.' But that also proved to be meaningless"* (Ecclesiastes 2:1).

Success is more than *power*. Some people think success is climbing the ladder to the top. They'll climb over everybody they can to get to the top first. They'll even knock you off the ladder if you get in their way. Jesus had this problem in his own leadership group. James and John came to Jesus and asked Him if they could have the top two positions in Jesus' new administration in the kingdom of God.

"We want to sit at your right and left hand when you come into your kingdom," they said. The other disciples were furious. Why? Because James and John not only wanted to attain a position of prominence, they wanted to rule over the other disciples.

Jesus set them straight about the inherent evils of pursuing power for the purpose of ruling rather than serving. *"Whoever wants to become great among you must be your servant, and whoever wants to be first must be slave of all"* (Mark 10:43, 44).

Remember the adage, *Power corrupts; absolute power corrupts absolutely.* When Harry Truman was thrust into the presidency by the death of Franklin Delano Roosevelt, a friend took him aside and gave him some sound advice: "From here on out, you're going to have lots of people around you. They'll try to put up a wall around you and cut you off from any ideas but theirs. They'll tell you what a great man you are, Harry. But you and I both know you ain't."

Don't get me wrong. There is nothing wrong with being recognized for your accomplishments. I hope you are. Neither is there anything wrong with getting rich and prospering financially in your line of work. I trust you will. And there is nothing wrong with enjoying the good things of life that God has given us. Still, there is nothing wrong with holding a position of great importance.

There is a proper place for all these things in our lives. But there's much more to success than having fame, fortune, pleasure or position. We need a spiritual ingredient to keep it all in balance.

My father has always been a common sense thinker. He use to collect various quotes, anecdotes and newspaper clippings on success. When I graduated from high school and prepared to leave home for college, he gave me a newspaper article he had kept for many years. It is entitled, "With the World By the Tail."

In 1923, eight of the world's most successful financiers sat down at a business meeting. Present were: The president of the largest independent steel company. The president of the largest utility. The greatest wheat speculator. The president of the New York Stock Exchange. A member of the President's cabinet. The greatest "bear" on Wall Street. The president of the Bank of International Settlements. The head of the world's greatest monopoly.

These men controlled more wealth than is in the U.S. Treasury. Newspapers and magazines printed their success stores and urged the youth of the nation to follow their examples. Yet 25 years later, this is what happened to them:

The president of the steel company — Charles Schwab — lived on borrowed money for five years before he died bankrupt.

The president of the greatest utility empire — Samuel Insull — fled the country in disgrace to avoid prosecution.

The greatest wheat speculator — Arthur Cutter — died abroad insolvent.

The president of the NYSE — Richard Whitney — was sentenced to Sing Sing prison for larceny.

The member of the President's cabinet — Albert Fall — was pardoned from prison so he could die at home.

The greatest "bear" on Wall Street — Jesse Livermore — died a suicide.

The president of the International Bank —
Leon Frazer — died a suicide.
   The head of the greatest monopoly — Ivar
Krueger — died a suicide.
   All of these men learned well the art of money
making, but not one of them learned how to live.

Success is based on the important relationships in your life. It starts with your relationship to God. This relationship will determine everything else about your life — your attitudes, values, beliefs, philosophy of life and lifestyle. Here's the greatest commandment: *"Love the Lord your God with all your heart, soul and strength"* (Deuteronomy 6:5).

Jesus put it another way: *"Seek first the kingdom of God and His righteousness; and all these things shall be added unto you"* (Matthew 6:33). The whole reason God created us is for a relationship with Him. If we miss out on that, we've miss out on the purpose of our very existence.

Think about it — the greatest motivation for success is to strive to do everything for the glory of God. If you work to achieve your own glory you will waste your life. If you live for the glory of God, Jesus will reward you with eternal success and blessing. You will hear

Him say, *"Well done, good and faithful servant!"* (Matthew 25:21).

Let me ask you, what is the highest purpose for which you can live? Is it not to live and work, and love and play in such a way that brings glory to God? *"Whatever you do, do it all for the glory of God"* (1 Corinthians 10:31). The most important issue to consider in every area of life — *Does it glorify God?*

Second to your relationship to God are your relationships with others. Our relationships either make us or break us. The better our relationships, the more success we will achieve. The ability to communicate, to resolve conflict, to present ourselves in a positive way, and get along with others determines largely how successful we become. The ability to relate well to others can compensate for any lack of talent, ability or skill. You'll be amazed at how far you will go in life if you can get people to like you and to enjoy working with you.

Let's be honest about it, no one enjoys being around negative, cynical people who are jealous of others, who don't have a dream for their own lives and who always tell you why something *can't* be done. But everyone loves to be around positive people who are heading somewhere in life and always see opportunities instead of problems.

If you're going to succeed you'll have to build bridges into the hearts of people. Nobody succeeds alone. So, practice faithfully the second greatest commandment and the sky is the limit: *"Love your neighbor as yourself"* (Leviticus 19:10).

Zig Ziglar says, "You can get everything in life you want if you help enough people get what they want." You know you're successful when the people around you are better off because of their relationship with you.

Denis Waitely calls this *the double win.* In his book *The Double Win,* he takes issue with the law of the jungle, which is so pervasive in America. Winning is more than the survival of the fittest which states that for every winner there must be a loser. The ideas of succeeding and serving are incompatible in the law of the jungle. The motto is, Do it to others before they do it to you.

He offers a new strategy rather than the old win-lose model. I can win, and help you win at the same time. While I'm climbing the ladder of success, I will take you with me to the top. That's what he calls the double-win: *If I help you win, I win, too.*[1]

Several years ago a new breed of horses was tested

in Canada. Researchers found that one horse could pull an eight-ton load. When they teamed two horses together they anticipated that the horses would pull 16 or 18 tons. To their surprise, the team pulled a 30-ton load! This is the principle of synergism.

The law of synergism states that two or more objects working together can produce a greater effect than the objects working independently of each other. When you work with others to achieve your goals, you will multiply your results at an exponential rate of return.

Several years ago an unusual event occurred at the Special Olympics in Seattle. Nine mentally and physically handicapped runners took their places at the starting line of the 400-meter race. The race began and they ran as hard and fast as they could. About half way through the race one boy fell. He got up and started to run again. Then he fell again.

This time he lay there and started to cry. The other runners heard him and one by one they stopped running and went back to help him. They picked him up and all of them had to give him a reassuring hug. Then they joined hands and finished the race together.

The crowd and the judges were puzzled. Who won the race? After deliberation, the judges decided to award all nine runners the gold medal.

That's real success: *I only win when I help you win too.*

Finally, there is the relationship to the self. Successful people have a positive self-image with a realistic view of their strengths and weaknesses. In short, you have to like yourself if you expect others to like you. You need both God-confidence and self-confidence — faith in God and faith in yourself — in order to succeed.

Did you know that people who reject themselves feel rejected by others? It's true. People pick up on the way we feel about ourselves and then project those feelings back to us. If you believe in yourself, others will believe in you. If you exude self-confidence, others will put confidence in you. Conversely, if you reject yourself, others will reject you.

You're only ready for success when you truly accept and respect who you are. The greatest struggle we all have is the struggle for self-acceptance and self-respect. Justice Oliver Wendell Holmes said, "Most people die with their music still in them." You have incredible, untapped potential. You are made in the image of God.

God created you with the potential for greatness. Unfortunately, we get caught in the Charlie Brown syndrome. One day Charlie Brown was talking with Linus about his feelings of inadequacy. "You see, Linus," Charlie moaned, "it goes all the way back to the beginning. The moment I was born and set foot on the stage of life they took one look at me and said, 'Not right for the part.'"

The truth is, you are right for the part. God has given you a part to play in life. So, play it well. God is counting on you. And so are we. Besides, God believes in you, or else He wouldn't have created you. It's time for you to start believing in yourself.

Jesus took twelve of the most unlikely men, transformed them from fishermen, tax collectors and political zealots, into an army of leaders who made the greatest spiritual impact in history. How did Jesus do it? Simple — in the company of sinners He dreamed of saints. He convinced them they were capable of achieving more with their lives than they ever dreamed possible. And you know what? They did. They not only believed in Him — they believed in themselves.

Be true to yourself. Don't get trapped trying to be somebody else or, trying to live up to everyone's expectations. Besides, they probably don't expect nearly as much from you as you think. Shakespeare gave one of the greatest secrets to success and happiness: "To thine own self be true."

Successful people are sincere. They're true to themselves. They don't wear masks or play a part to be accepted. They are the genuine article. Sincerity comes from two Latin words *sine* and *cera*, meaning, "to be without wax." It comes from ancient times when merchants of pottery would fill the cracks of pottery with wax so that patrons would not detect the flaws. Wise shoppers, however, would lift a piece of pottery and hold it up to the light of the sun. The rays would shine through any flaws hidden with wax.

Now we are ready for a definition of success. Read it aloud: *Success means to love God with all my heart and to be faithful to what He has called me to do in life; to help bring out the best in others as I seek to win in every endeavor; and to value who I am, as a unique individual made in the image of God and to strive to reach my highest potential in life for the glory of God.*

Reference

Denis Waitley, *The Double Win* (Old Tappan: Revell, 1985).

DIRECTION

"Joseph had a dream..."
Genesis 37:5

Do you remember the biblical story of Joseph? He was the young man whose father gave him the famous coat of many colors. He also was a man with a dream. One day Joseph's brothers saw him approaching and said, "Here comes that dreamer!" (Genesis 37:19).

They meant it as a criticism. It was really a great compliment. If you are going to succeed, you need a dream. People need to say about you, *Here comes that dreamer!*

Dreams only become reality when we make the right decisions. Life is a matter of choice not chance. Every decision is based on two fundamental questions. Remember to ask and answer these fundamental questions before making any major decision:

Where are you going?

How do you plan to get there?

The first question, Where are you going? has to do with direction and purpose. You need a dream for your life. Martin Luther King rallied the civil rights movement behind one clarion call, "I have a dream!"

We use the word dream in a variety of ways. When we think of dreams we usually think of dreams in the night. But dreams are also visions, goals and aspirations.

George Bernard Shaw said, "Some men see things and say why? But I dream of things that never were and I say, why not?"

An IRS publication misquoted Shaw: "Some men see things as they are and say why? I dread things that never were and say why not?"

Your dreams determine the quality of your life. *"As a man thinks in his heart so is he"* (Proverbs 23:7). Without a dream, you will drift aimlessly through life reacting to one circumstance after another. Each day you live will seem disconnected from the other robbing your life of purpose.

Without a dream, we lack a master plan by which to build our lives. Proverbs 29:18 reminds us, *"Where there is no vision, there the people perish."* Can you imagine trying to build a house without a set of construction plans? It would be utter chaos. If you're like me and have lived through the process of building a house, you know it can be chaos even with plans much less without them.

When you have a dream for your life you will live each day with a sense of purpose. Every day you live will become another piece in a beautiful mosaic that God and you are making together. God will give you a dream for your life just like He did for Joseph. And people will say of you, "Here comes that dreamer!"

Dreams possess power. Walter Fauntroy, former delegate to the House of Representatives for the District of Columbia, delivered a speech at Howard University, in which he said: *"The past is yours, learn from it. The present is yours, fulfill it. The future is yours, preserve it. Knowledge is yours, use it. Cancer is yours, cure it. Racism is yours, end it...Do not be blinded by prejudice, disheartened by the times or discouraged by the system...Do not let anything paralyze your mind, tie your hands, or defeat your spirit. Take the world not to dominate it, but to deliver it; not to exploit it, but to enrich it — take the dream and inherit the earth."*

Remember two powerful truths about dreams. First, *dream while you are young.* The years of childhood and adolescence are crucial years for developing a dream for life. Did you know that two-thirds of people who become Christians make that decision before they reach age 18? And most people who decide to enter Christian service as a career and calling do so before they reach age 21.

You don't have to wait until you're older before you start dreaming. Start dreaming now! Raphael painted his works at a very young age and died at 37. Alfred Tennyson wrote his first work at 18. Victor Hugo was only 17 when he received prizes at a poetry competition and earned the title "master" before he was 20.

John Calvin joined the Reformation at 21 and at 27 wrote *The Institutes of the Christian Religion.* Isaac Newton was 24 when he formulated the law of gravity and made some of his greatest discoveries before he was 25. Charles Dickens wrote *Pickwick Papers* at 24 and *Oliver Twist* at 25.

Charles Spurgeon was a powerful preacher in his early 20s and by age 25, pastored the largest church in London. Martin Luther King shook the nation with his call for civil rights while he was still a young man before being cut down in the prime of his life. And don't forget that Jesus Himself had transformed the course of human history by the time He was 33.

Second, *keep dreaming regardless of your age.* The prophet said, *"Your old men will dream dreams"* (Joel

GROOM/TRACY
DOE 10-18-10

BOARDING PASS

FLIGHT DL1918   DATE 09OCT   CLASS F   ORIGIN ORLANDO INTL

OPERATED BY DELTA AIR LINES INC   COACH   DESTINATION ATLANTA

DEPARTURE GATE 73   **SUBJECT TO CHANGE**

NRSA   HAV6W5

DEPARTS 230P   BRD TIME 150P

SEAT 29B   ZONE 4

BAGS 01

MC09CE323/0D

GROOM/TRACY
DOE 10-18-10

BOARDING PASS

FLIGHT DL1918   DATE 09OCT

ORIGIN ORLANDO INTL

DESTINATION ATLANTA

OPERATED BY DELTA AIR LINES INC

SEAT 29B   ZONE 4

BAGS 01

2:28). It has been said that a man is never old until regrets take the place of his dreams. It's okay to retire from your job, but never retire from living. Don't be like the man who wrote:

I get up each morning, dust off my wits, Pick up the paper, and read the obits.

If my name is missing, I know I'm not dead, So I eat a good breakfast — and go back to bed.

You're younger than you think! Moses was eighty when God called him to lead Israel out of Egypt. Michangelo was writing poetry and designing architecture until the time he died. He painted the ceiling of the Sistine Chapel on his back on a scaffold at nearly ninety. Goethe wrote a part of *Faust* at age 60 and finished it at 82.

Daniel Webster wrote his monumental dictionary when he was 70. Verdi produced the famous piece "Ave Maria" at 85. John Wesley preached for 40 years, produced 400 books, knew ten languages and at age 86 complained that he was unable to preach more than twice a day. I have a close friend whose father received his doctorate at the young age of 76. So, keep on dreaming!

Now that you know where you want to go, you're

ready to tackle the second question, How do you plan to get there? It takes concrete goals to make dreams come true.

Here's a workable action plan for setting and reaching your goals.

Step #1 — Personalize. The most important goals in life concern your personal development. God is more concerned with who you are than what you do. Virtuous goals will make you a better person as you reach them.

Let's be honest on this point. What good is it if you become a millionaire at the expense of your happiness, health or family? What good is it if you achieve success in athletics, academics or business at the expense of compromising your convictions? Many people have attained certain levels of success only to have become worse human beings in the process.

So, before you set goals for your family, business, education, career advancement or any other worthwhile endeavor, set personal goals for your own spiritual development and emotional maturity. After all, who you are is more important that what you do.

Step #2 — Prioritize. Distinguish between the urgent and the important. Time management is crucial to reaching goals. Jesus said, *"Seek first the kingdom of God"*

(Matthew 6:33). In other words, put first things first.

Start by making a list of your *top five priorities* in life. Then, make a list of the *five most important people* in your life. These are the people you need to spend quality time with if you're going to succeed.

Next, make a list of the *top five priorities of your weekly schedule.* Make sure you accomplish these tasks each week. Don't allow urgent demands on your schedule to keep you from fulfilling your responsibilities.

Finally, make a list of the *five most important goals* you want to achieve in life. Take time to review your weekly, monthly and annual calendar. Are you devoting the necessary time to these priorities in order to make your dreams a reality?

When you have successfully identified the most important people in your life, the most important tasks you have to perform and the most important accomplishments you would like to make, you are well on your way to success. Invest your time in these people, tasks and accomplishments. Remember this simple rule: *20 percent of your efforts will produce 80 percent of your results.*

Use your time wisely. Invest it in what is important and refuse to be driven by the urgent. Workaholics do not get more done than others. They just burn out faster.

Don't work harder, work smarter through wise planning.

Every day God gives us the gift of time — 24 hours, 1,440 minutes or 86,400 seconds. Time is a unique commodity. You can spend it, you can waste it, but you can't save it. Time passes quickly. It waits for no one.

The great enemy to using our time wisely is procrastination. The word procrastination comes from two Latin words, *pros* meaning forward and *cras* meaning tomorrow. Some people take Mark Twain's humor seriously, "Never put off until tomorrow what you can put off until the day after tomorrow."

Here's a strategy for making the most of your time:

1. *Begin every year with an annual plan.* I use the Christmas and New Year's holidays to plan my calendar for the upcoming year. Believe me, it will give you an incredible sense of control over your time and a clear sense of what you plan to accomplish for the year. Take an annual calendar and write down all the important dates and times for meetings, vacations and special projects. Write every *important* event on your annual calendar. This will keep your energies focused on what is important rather than reacting to all the urgent demands on your time.

2. *Review and organize specific dates and times of*

events each month. Review the upcoming month at the beginning of each month. Make sure you balance out your time so that it is invested in the important people and the important tasks. If you find you haven't, then make the necessary adjustments on your calendar.

3. *Review your calendar weekly.* Take time every weekend to review your schedule for the upcoming week. Make sure you haven't over committed yourself on certain projects and meetings. If you have, make appropriate adjustments on Monday for the upcoming week. If you are going to get a handle on your time you will have to learn the fine art of saying no. You can't do everything asked of you if you expect to reach your goals. Stay focused on who and what is really important to you.

4. *Every day needs to be guided by the daily calendar of activities and appointments.* If it is a workday your schedule needs to be detailed to keep you on track. If you are taking a day off, then write a mark through the day and designate it as such. I suggest that you develop your daily calendar the night before each day rather than waiting until the morning. If you wait too late in your planning each day you'll find yourself driven by the tyranny of the urgent hurrying from

one appointment to the next.

Reviewing the daily calendar the evening before enables you to make any necessary adjustments to the schedule. You will also awake with your thoughts focused on the day ahead because it has been thoughtfully prepared. You will face the day with enthusiasm and peace because you are prepared. (By the way, most days will already be prepared if you have already completed your calendar with annual, monthly and weekly events and responsibilities.)

Step #3 — Pray. Submit all your goals to the will of God. Make it your ambition in life to fulfill the Lord's Prayer: *"Your kingdom come, your will be done."* You will find that as you pray God will give you goals and plans for your life. Prayer is God's pathway to creative planning and peaceful living. Peace is the fruit of believing prayer. God will guide your life as He speaks to you in prayer.

Take time to sit quietly in the presence of God. *"In quietness and trust is your strength"* (Isaiah 30:15). In solitude and quietness we hear God speak in the sanctuary of our souls. *"Whether you turn to the right or to the left, your ears will hear a voice behind you, saying, 'This is the way; walk in it'"* (Isaiah 30:21).

During a Super Bowl, a Dallas Cowboy's lineman

recovered a fumble and began dancing on his way to the end zone. But he had the ball stripped from his hand at the goal line and failed to score the touchdown. His name was Leon Lett, and the moral of the story is, "Don't Lett Up!"

Jesus said, *"Always pray and never give up"* (Luke 18:1). Prayer is our lifeline to God. Without it we are left powerless to meet life's demands and pressures. But when we pray we become larger than life.

Step #4 — Plan. As you write out your goals, follow these five rules:

1. *Goals need to be specific.* The best way to specify your goals is to write them down. Goals that are not written down are seldom accomplished.

2. *Goals need to be realistic.* There's no need in trying to be the next Pavoroti if you can't carry a tune in a bucket. Go for the goals that are within your reach.

3. *Goals are both short-range and long-range.* Make a list of both short-range goals, say within a five-year period, and goals that are in the back of your mind for some time down the road. Life moves in seasons. Dream now about what you would like to do in the next season of life.

4. *Goals need to be flexible.* Goals need to be reevaluated and revised periodically. Life-situations

change, which warrant the readjustment of goals. For example, financial portfolios need to reviewed and sometimes modified at least once a year.

5. *Goals need to be measurable.* Monitor your progress. Keep a written record so you can see how far you've come toward reaching your goals.

Step #5 — Prize. Whenever you reach a goal, reward yourself for a job well done. Go out and do something you enjoy. Celebrate your successes. We spend too much time punishing ourselves for our mistakes and not enough time rewarding our successes.

Step #6 — Participate. Involve others in the process. Share your goals with the important people in your life. Ask them to pray for you, to hold you accountable in reaching your goals, and to give you feedback on your progress. The Bible says, *"Two are better than one, because they have a good return for their work: If one falls down, his friend can help him up. But pity the man who falls and has no one to help him up!"* (Ecclesiastes 4:9,10).

Don Bennet is a Seattle businessman who decided to climb Washington's Mount Rainer. The summit reaches 14,410 feet. While many people have made the climb, for Don it was an incredible accomplishment. His story made national headlines. Don Bennet was the first amputee to make the climb. He made the climb on one leg and two crutches.

Asked by a reporter what was the greatest lesson he learned from his achievement, he talked about his team who helped him reach his goal. He said, "I learned that you can't do it alone." So it is with life. You can't do it alone. We need the power of God to make it. And we need others to help us reach our goals.

Step #7 — *Persevere.* When you are on the right path, pursuing the right goals, then stick to your plan. Never give up. Never say, "I quit." Take those words out of your vocabulary. Perseverance declares confidently, *"I press on for the mark"* (Philippians 3:14).

Barbie and I have tried to instill in our children that the two most important ingredients of success are hard work and perseverance. Finish what you start. Don't stop short of your goals.

After being expelled from college, Duke Rudman drifted into jobs in Texas oil fields. As he gained experience, he dreamed of independent oil exploration. Whenever he would get a few thousand dollars together, he leased drilling equipment and sank a well. He drilled 29 wells in two years and came up dry every time.

At age forty, he remained unsuccessful. He began studying land formations, shale types and other aspects of geology to improve his chances. He leased his 30th tract of land and this time a large oil reservoir was discovered.

Still, 75 percent of the wells he drills are dry. After some sixty years of drilling for oil, he says he believes he has failed more than anyone in the business. But he struck oil enough times to earn $220 million. "There were days I wanted to quit," says Rudman, "but I'd just push the thought away and get back to work."

You too can succeed in every endeavor of life when you have a clear vision of where you want to go and how you plan to get there. Stick to your plan. Eventually, you too will strike oil. So, push back every negative thought and get back to work.

DESIRE

"For to me, to live is Christ and to die is gain."
Philippians 1:21

When you get right down to it, people basically do in life what they want to do. That may sound too direct, but it's true. The key to success is channeling our desires into worthwhile goals and ambitions.

Apathy is a major enemy to success. Successful people never say, "I don't care." Or, "I'm doing just as little as I can get by with." Although America is a land of opportunity and enjoys its finest hour of economic success, many individuals lack any real desire to better their lifestyle or their standard of living. In short, they have no passion for life. They talk about being bored, unconcerned and just wanting to get by with as little hassle as possible.

Helen Keller made an interesting observation about human nature: "Science may have found a cure for most evils; but it has found no remedy for the worst of them all — the apathy of human beings."

Apathy starts with self-preoccupation. We get so wrapped up in ourselves and in getting what we want that we lose our concern for others. After we've had our fill of spending everything we make on ourselves, we get bored. That's why every person needs a cause greater than himself for which to live. Success means living outside yourself.

"Life is a place of service," Leo Tolstoy said. "Joy can be real only if people look upon their life as a service and have a definite object in life outside themselves and their personal happiness."

Apathy also results from feeling overly satisfied with our accomplishments. Like the people at Laodicea we say, *"I'm rich; I have acquired much wealth and do not need a thing"* (Revelation 3:17). It's easy to fall asleep in the lap of luxury. When times are good, people tend to lose their edge and grow lax.

Thomas Carlyle, Scottish essayist, said, "For every person who can handle prosperity there are a hundred who can handle adversity." That may sound odd to you, but consider what he means. It takes more character to handle good times than it does to endure bad times.

Homer, the Greek poet, observed, "Adversity has the effect of eliciting talents which in prosperous circumstances would have lain dormant." You are like a teabag — you will never know what you're made of until you're in hot water!

Apathy also results from stress overload and burnout. Now, not all stress is bad. We need proper amounts of stress to keep us motivated. Without it, we rust out. But too much stress causes us to burn out. The American Association of Family Physicians reports that two-thirds of office visits to family doctors are about stress related and stress-induced problems.

A *USA Today* article pointed out that stress is not only a problem in America, it is a global phenomenon. Stress related health problems such as ulcers, high blood pressure and heart attacks cost the American economy $200 billion dollars a year in absenteeism, insurance claims and medical costs.

Stress is a state of mental, emotional and physical tension. When we get stressed-out we lose our enthusiasm and our motivation. Life comes to a grinding halt. We can barely muster up enough energy to get out of bed every morning and get to work. Stress overload leaves us fatigued, feeling like we're running on empty. We lose our desire and passion.

So, how can we get the fire back?

First, *refocus your energy on your goals*. Sit down and write out your plan of action. Get your life back on track. Quit being driven by the tyranny of the urgent and get back to doing in life what is important.

Second, *replenish your spiritual and emotional resources*. Don't allow yourself to run on empty too long. Take a mini-vacation. Go to church. Read a good motivational book. You have to feed your mind and heart just like you do your body. Inner renewal is the antidote to burnout.

Third, *renew your hope*. I once read that hope is the confident expectation based on certain fundamental truths and actions. For me, those fundamental truths and actions are the promises of God. I've learned that if you ask God, He will give you a new vision for your life.

Learn about the dreams of others. Their dreams will inspire you to dream. Hope simply means that your life can change. There's a better day coming. Tomorrow's possibilities are unlimited.

Orison Marden, editor for *Success* magazine (1848-1924) said, "There is no medicine like hope, no incentives so great, and no tonics so powerful as the expectation of something better tomorrow."

After our workout at the fitness center, a friend said to me, "Hey, pastor, give me a Bible verse to think about today." We had just finished playing basketball for an hour and a half. (And, believe me, you need a positive thought from God's Word after that.)

I thought for a moment and said, "Here's your verse for today — Jeremiah 29:11."

He got his Bible out of his locker and read it. "That's a fantastic verse," he said. "That will carry me through the day." It reads: *"'For I know the plans I have for you', declares the Lord, 'plans to prosper you and not to harm you, plans to give you a hope and a future.'"*

You have to pursue the plan of God for your life with passion. No one will reach your goals or fulfill your dreams for you. Remember, *If it's to be, it's up to me.*

I heard about a man's grandfather who came to America from Europe and after being processed at Ellis Island, went into a cafeteria in New York City to get something to eat. He sat down at an empty table and waited for someone to take his order. Of course, nobody ever did.

Finally, a man with a tray full of food sat down opposite him and told him how things worked. "Start at the end" he said, "and just go along and pick out what you want. At the other end they'll tell you how much you have to pay for it."

"I soon learned that's how everything works in America," the man said. "Life is a cafeteria. You can get anything you want as long as you're willing to pay the price. You can even get success. But you'll never get it if you wait for someone to bring it to you. You have to get up and get it yourself."

Success belongs to those who really want it. You have to get up and get it for yourself. Nobody can achieve success for you. Even Jesus said, *"Blessed are those who hunger and thirst for righteousness, for they will be filled"* (Matthew 5:6).

I recall a television interview with Arnold Schwartzeneggar conducted by Barbara Walters. He won the Mr. Universe title eight consecutive times and went on to a successful acting career. She asked him, "Do you have a philosophy of life?" He replied with a big smile—"Stay hungry."

One day a young man came to Socrates desiring to be tutored by the great philosopher. "I want to acquire knowledge," he told Socrates. Socrates told him to meet him tomorrow down by the lake. When the young man arrived the next day, Socrates led him out into the lake.

Then suddenly, Socrates grabbed him by the head and plunged him under the water. He held him down until the young man thought he would drown. Finally, he let him up. He sprang out of the water, gasping for air. After catching his breath, he demanded angrily, "Why did you do that? I could have drowned!"

Socrates asked, "What did you want more than anything else when I held you under the water?"

The young man replied, "I wanted air!"

Socrates said, "When you want knowledge as much as you wanted air, you will get it."

That's the kind of passion and desire it takes to achieve success. Guard yourself against apathy and keep the fire burning. *"Never be lacking in zeal, but keep your spiritual fervor, serving the Lord"* (Romans 12:11).

DISCIPLINE

"The spirit is willing, but the body is weak."
Matthew 26:41

Whether we like it or not, success requires discipline. Webster says that discipline is the training of our mental, moral and physical powers by instruction, control and exercise. Athletes are well acquainted with the importance of discipline.

The apostle Paul used athletic metaphors to stress the need of discipline: *"Do you not know that in a race all the runners run, but only one gets the prize? Run in such a way as to get the prize. Everyone who competes in the games goes into strict training. They do it to get a crown that will not last; but we do it to get a crown that will last forever. Therefore, I do not run like a man running aimlessly; I do not fight like a man beating the air. No, I beat my body and make it my slave so that after I have preached to others, I myself will not be disqualified for the prize"* (1 Corinthians 9:24-27).

Parents discipline their children so that children learn how to discipline their own lives. Undisciplined children grow up to be undisciplined adults. Discipline is a matter of being in control of one's life and being responsible for one's actions.

Now don't make the mistake of trying to control others, or even circumstances. You can't. But there are some things you can control. Denis Waitley, in *Seeds of Greatness,* gives seven C's of control:

We control the *clock*, the way we use our time and organize our schedule.

We control our *concepts*, how we think and our attitudes toward life.

We control our *contacts*, the people we spend time with and those who influence us.

We control our *communication*, what we say or don't say and how well we listen and understand others.

We control our *commitments*, the ways we invest our time, energy and money.

We control our *causes*, the spiritual and community service endeavors which add meaning to our lives.

We control our *concerns*, those things we tend

to worry about.

Here's an axiom I try to live by: *Control the things you can control, and leave the rest to God.*

Successful people practice **moral and spiritual discipline.** We live in a chaotic society because many people indulge every desire. The Bible records the tragic epics of those who failed to discipline their desires. Cain failed to discipline his anger and murdered his brother. Esau failed to discipline his appetite and sold his birthright. Lot failed to discipline the lust of his eyes and coveted the plains of Sodom.

Samson failed to discipline his passions and lost his power. King Saul failed to discipline his quest for power and lost his throne. King David failed to discipline his desires and was unfaithful to God. Judas failed to discipline his self-interests and betrayed Christ with a kiss.

Pilate failed to discipline his political aspirations and washed his hands of Jesus, even though he knew Jesus was innocent. The disciples failed to discipline their fears and deserted Jesus at His trial.

The Book of Judges chronicles a dark period of Israeli history. It was a time marked by spiritual decline and social degradation brought on by the lack of discipline. The writer simply says: *"Everyone did as he saw fit"* (Judges 21:24). No law. No accountability to God or others. No moral boundaries. No absolutes. As a result, chaos reigned.

Oscar Wilde came to America for a visit in 1882. When asked by the Customs Agent if he had anything to declare he boasted, "Only my genius."

Fifteen years later, alone and broken in prison, he reflected on his life of waste and excess. He wrote: "I have been a spendthrift of my genius...I forgot that every little action of the common day makes or un-makes character." He failed to discipline his desires.

Achieving success also requires **physical discipline**. No one learns how to discipline the inner life of the spirit and the mind, until they first learn to discipline the body through proper rest, balanced nutrition and regular exercise.

Research on sleep deprivation shows that most people need nine hours of rest each night for maximum efficiency. (Now you know why you're so tired.) Sleep deprivation is related to depression, mood swings, fatigue, lack of concentration, anger and rage reactions and memory loss.

Physical discipline requires healthy nutrition. Proper eating increases physical energy and mental alertness.

The Old Testament Levitical code outlined important dietary guidelines for the Israelites. Modern medicine has verified the wisdom of these ancient dietary laws. Dr. S. I. Macmillan explores the value of the Levitical dietary and medical laws in his classic work, *None of These Diseases.*

Establish a consistent exercise routine. Now you don't have to look like Arnold Swartzeneggar or Suzanne Sommers. But you must take exercise seriously. The quality of your life depends on it. Aerobic exercise and weightlifting increases heart rate, lowers blood pressure, combats arthritis and osteoporosis, strengthens muscles, relieves stress, lowers anxiety and improves one's attitude toward life. People who exercise regularly not only feel better, they feel better about themselves.

Let's face it — we're all getting older. So we need to take good care of ourselves. And don't wait until it's too late to start exercising and eating right. Talking about getting older reminds me of some choice philosophy on aging someone sent me recently.

Comedian Milton Berle said, "The trouble with life is, by the time you can read a woman like a book, your library card has expired."

Don't take life so seriously — its not permanent.

Robert Benchley remarked, "As for me, except for an occasional heart attack, I feel as young as I ever did."

Someone astutely observed that, "The aging process could be slowed down if it went through Congress."

According to Mickey Rooney, "Age is nothing but experience, and some of us are more experienced than others."

Finally, here's a helpful Last Will and Testament: "Being of sound mind, I spent all my money."

We also need to develop **emotional discipline**. It's not what we're eating but what's eating us that causes most our problems. Mark Twain said, "I've suffered through many troubles in life. Most of which have never happened."

Everyone battles worry. Worry is an anxious, troubled or fearful state of mind. Someone has said that worry is thinking with our emotions. Worriers experience the phenomenon of the "racing mind" characterized by an endless stream of anxious thoughts.

Worry results in increased muscle tension, eating disorders, anxiety and depression, which, in turn, leads to more serious health problems. Chronic worriers often suffer from low self-esteem.

The Greek word for worry means to be divided or inwardly distracted. The worried mind is a divided mind — a mind torn between faith and fear. The English word worry actually comes from an Anglo-Saxon word meaning to choke or strangle. Worry chokes out our hopes, dreams and aspirations leaving us trapped in a prison of fear.

Here's a beatitude worth remembering: *Blessed is the man who is too busy to worry during the day, and too sleepy to worry at night.*

We often worry about what other people think of us. I once read that at age 20, we worry about what others think of us. At age 40, we don't care what they think of us. At age 60, we discover they haven't been thinking about us at all!

My older brother Bill is a successful entrepreneur in Atlanta. He is president and founder of a company in computer-based technology. He began his business about the same time I started my first church. We both started with limited resources. We both had big dreams for the future. The only difference was I worried about failing but he didn't.

So, one day I asked him, "Bill, what would you do

if your company went bankrupt?" I thought he would disclose to me his hidden fears about going out on a limb financially to start his own business.

But he didn't. Nonchalantly, he replied, "I would just start over and build another business." His calmness and confidence was sincere. I decided to adopt his attitude from that day on.

We don't try to succeed because we're afraid of failure. So, you may need this powerful axiom for facing fear when it comes knocking on the door of your heart: *Fear knocked at the door. Faith answered. There was no one there.*

Fear asks, What if? What if you fail? What if you go bankrupt? What if you can't finish what you started? What if you get sick? What if...? We are haunted with the what ifs of life.

Faith answers, *I can do all things through Christ who gives me strength!* (Philippians 4:13). You have to know beyond a shadow of a doubt that you can and you will succeed. You and God constitute a majority. Together you can overcome any obstacle to your success. I have learned that failure is not your big threat. It's the fear of failure you have to look out for.

I once read that fear is *False Expectations Appearing Real.* President Roosevelt said so wisely in his inaugural address, in the wake of the Great Depression, "There's nothing to fear but fear itself."

And besides if you do fail it's not the end of the world. Everybody fails. The only people who never fail are the ones who never attempt anything. When Thomas Edison invented the light bulb, he tried over 2,000 experiments before he got it to work.

A young reporter asked him how it felt to fail so many times. He said, "I never failed once. I invented the light bulb. It just happened to be a 2,000-step process."

I stumbled on an obscure Bible verse one day that helped me bounce back from failure. The prophet Micah said, *"Though I have fallen, I will rise!"* (Micah 6:8). That's the attitude of a winner.

"Died of worry," Dr. John Haggai says in his excellent book, *How To Win Over Worry,* "could be written factually on many tombstones."

I once heard that if you don't bother God everything else will bother you. Here's how you fight worry. *"Do not be anxious about anything, but in everything, by prayer and petition, with thanksgiving, present your requests to God. And the peace of God, which transcends all understanding, will guard your hearts and your minds in Christ Jesus"* (Philippians 4:6, 7).

A French soldier in World War I used to carry this piece to help him overcome worry:

Of two things, one is certain. Either you are at the front, or you are behind the lines. If you are at the front, of two things, one is certain. Either you are exposed to danger or you are in a safe place. If you are exposed to danger, of two things one is certain. Either you are wounded or you are not wounded. If you are wounded, of two things one is certain. Either you recover, or you die. If you recover, there is no need to worry. If you die, you cannot worry. SO WHY WORRY?

Now, there are certainly areas of life we can't control. We can't control the thoughts or actions of others. We can't control accidents or tragedies, corporate downsizing, or personal illness. But we can choose our attitudes, values and beliefs. We can choose how we will respond to the adversities of life.

Victor Frankl, survivor of Hitler's death camps and a brilliant psychiatrist said, "The last and greatest of all human freedoms is the ability to choose one's own attitude in any given set of circumstances." He even learned to find meaning in suffering. That's exactly how he survived.

Max Lucado says, "If there are a thousand steps between us and God, he will take all but one. He will leave the final one for us. the choice is ours." You see, God does not force us to love and obey Him. The choice is ours.

When you learn to live by your choices instead of your feelings, you will be a victor instead of a victim. No one can succeed with a victim mentality. Victimization is public enemy number one in America today. To be sure there are real victims of our times — victims of crime, discrimination, and injustice.

Victimization, however, is an attitude that shrinks back from taking responsibility in life. The victim cries, "It's not my fault." The victim demands, "The world owes me a living." Today we have no-fault divorces, no-fault auto insurance, and now no-fault moral choices.

Jesse Jackson observed, "You are not responsible for being down, but you are responsible for getting up." What happens to you is not your fault. But what you do in response to what happens to you is your responsibility.

You make the choice — victim or a victor? Which will it be?

The victim says, "I can't"; the victor says, "I can do all things through Christ who gives me strength."

The victim says, "It's not my fault!"; the victor says, "I am responsible for my actions."

The victim says, "We never did it that way before"; The victor says, "Nothing ventured, nothing gained."

The victim lives in fear; the victor walks by faith.

The victim sees problems; the victor sees opportunities.

The victim strikes back; the victor turns the other cheek.

The victim harbors resentment; the victor forgives even as God has forgiven him.

The victim gives up; the victor presses on.

The victim explains why it can't be done; the victor believes it can be done.

The victim offers excuses; the victor sets an example.

The victim is reactive; the victor is proactive.

The victim says, "With man this is impossible"; the victor says, "With God all things are possible!"

The victim says, "The odds are against us"; the victor says, "If God be for us who can be against us?"

I've always been inspired by the life of Booker T. Washington. He used to carry the books of other children as they went to school. He was deprived of an education, although he longed to learn. Yet, when he was a young man he fulfilled his dream and got his education.

Washington put success into perspective: "Success is not measured by what one achieves in life but rather by the obstacles one overcomes in the achievement of that success." He refused to be a victim of discrimination. He was a victor.

There's a thought-provoking line in *Gone With The Wind*: "Ain't nothin' from the outside can lick any of us." You see, it's what is on the inside that defeats us — attitudes of fear, pessimism, resentment and negativism.

Helen Keller was a victor. Although blind and deaf, she refused to play the role of a victim. She shows us how to rise above victimization in her poem, "They Took Away."

They took away what should have been my
eyes; but I remembered Milton's Paradise.

They took away what should have been my
ears; Beethoven came and wiped away my tears.

They took away what should have been my
tongue; But I talked with God when I was young.

He would not let them take away my soul;
possessing that I possessed the whole.

Before we leave this thought of being a victor, let

me share with you an incredible story of a high school graduate from the class of 2000 named Camara Barrett. He was valedictorian and first in his class when he graduated from Thomas Jefferson High School in Brooklyn. He was also Class President, editor of the school paper, a peer tutor, and an award-winning public speaker. And he worked 15 hours a week at a Brooklyn medical center.

So, it's no surprise that he got admitted to eight universities and is going to Cornell University on a scholarship. The surprise is that he achieved all this while living in a homeless shelter. After a bitter conflict with his parents, he found himself out on the street. For four days, he lived and studied on the subway at night, getting off to go to school during the day.

After the people at Thomas Jefferson helped Camara get settled in a homeless shelter, he pulled his grades back up, studied diligently for his SATs, and applied for college. Rather than destroying him, the experience of being alone strengthened his resolve to study and to do something with his life. His was a victor instead of a victim.

These are the true heroes of our day. Not the movie stars, teen idols and sports heroes. Heroes like Booker T. Washinton, Helen Keller and Camara Barrett inspire us, and especially young people, to transcend adversity, discrimination and disabilities to achieve our highest potential through the power of a disciplined life.

References

Denis Waitley, *Seeds of Greatness* (Old Tappan: Revell, 1983), 77.

DETERMINATION

*"I press on toward the goal to win the prize for which
God has called me heavenward in Christ Jesus."*
Philippians 3:14

Success boils down to hanging on when you feel like letting go. In the comic strip *Peanuts,* Lucy is in her psychiatrist's booth giving counsel to Charlie Brown who has just lost another baseball game. He's depressed and defeated.

Lucy says, "Look, Chuck, you just have to face the fact that life is a series of ups and downs."

He goes away screaming, "I hate downs — all I want is ups!"

Don't kid yourself. You're going to have some down times. So, determine to make it through the down times before they come. To be determined means to reach a decision, to have a fixed purpose and to maintain a firm resolve.

I need to point out that determination does not

mean to keep doing something if it's not working. I've seen individuals persist in business plans, financial strategies and personal goals that weren't working. So, remember it's okay to quit when you realize you have the wrong plan. That's not being a quitter; that's being smart.

When you're on the right path and you've got the right plan, stick with it until you reach your goals.

Fight through opposition.

Bounce back from setbacks.

Persevere through disappointment.

Get up when you fall.

Make up your mind to succeed.

There's a statement in the Gospel of Luke about Jesus, which stirs my heart: *"Jesus resolutely set out for Jerusalem* (Luke 9:51). The word *resolutely* literally means, he "set his face like a flint." He was immovable in his direction and purpose. Jerusalem meant rejection and eventually, death.

His own disciples tried to prevent him from going to Jerusalem. They knew the risk he was taking. Still, He resolutely set out for Jerusalem. He was the epitome of dedication to the will of God.

The question is, what have you resolutely set out to accomplish with your life with such determination that you cannot be dissuaded?

Remember, *it's not what you feel, it's what you will* that brings success. Don't allow your emotions to rule your life. To be successful you will have to make choices based on what you *will* not on what you *feel*. We put too much emphasis on what we *feel* and not enough about what we *will*.

Successful people have learned to tap the power of personal responsibility. All through the Bible we read about individuals who transcended their feelings and persisted with their plans.

I'm sure Noah didn't feel like building an ark and being the laughingstock of the community; but he obeyed God, built the ark and saved his family.

Abraham didn't feel like taking Issac to Moriah; but he arose early in the morning and set out to the place God showed him and discovered that God will provide.

Moses didn't feel like going to Egypt and confronting Pharaoh; but he went in obedience and led Israel out of Egypt into the promises of God.

Deborah didn't feel like leading Israel as a prophetess and judge in a society dominated by male leadership; but she took the challenge and led her nation to victory.

David didn't feel like facing Goliath alone in battle;

but he took his sling along with five smooth stones and declared, "I come to you in the name of the Lord of hosts."

I'm sure Mary, the mother of Jesus, didn't feel like being chosen for the virgin birth. (Can you image trying to explain *that* to your fiancé, family and friends?) Yet, she said to the angel, "I am the Lord's servant. May it be to me as you have said."

Jesus didn't feel like going to Calvary; but for the joy set before Him he endured the cross and redeemed the world.

The apostle Paul didn't feel like preaching the gospel at the cost of rejection, imprisonment and eventually a martyr's death; but he declared, "I have fought a good fight, I have finished the course and I have kept the faith!"

When Olympic gymnast Kerri Strug was asked by her coach Bela Karolyi, if she could do the vault that helped earn the U.S. women a gold metal in team competition, she said, "Yes, I will, I will, I will."

Don't try to reach your goals by taking the path of least resistance. Avoid taking the easy road. If you want real success you'll have to count the cost and pay the price. As one country preacher said, "There ain't no shortcut to the Promised Land!"

If you were to visit Boston and study the road system, you might conclude that there was no master design at all to the roads. They wind around with no rhyme or reason. That's because the first roads were constructed along cow paths.

Cows take the path of least resistance. When cows walk up a hill they don't say, "Here's a hill. Let's navigate the best path possible." No, they simply follow the path of least resistance stepping around the next rock, or steep grade. When they return to the same area they simply follow the previous course, eventually beating down the grass and forming a path.

Stay off the path of least resistance. And don't allow anyone or anything to deter you from your course.

Success requires us to go beyond the initial excitement of a project and finish what we start. Enthusiasm must be tempered with determination for dreams to become reality. The main difference between success and failure lies in the ability to finish what you start. The world is filled with starters but lacking in finishers.

Ignace Paderewski was a famous concert pianist and prime minister. A mother wanting to encourage her young son's progress on the piano, bought tickets to a Paderewski performance. Arriving at the concert they found that their tickets were near the front of the stage. They eyed the majestic Steinway waiting on stage. While the mother was talking to a friend, her son slipped away in the crowd.

When the concert began, the spotlights came on. The audience became quiet. Suddenly everyone noticed the little boy sitting at the piano innocently picking out "Twinkle, Twinkle, Little Star."

The mother was horrified. Then the master appeared on stage. "Don't quit — keep playing," he said to the boy. Leaning over him, Paderewski reached down his left hand and started playing a bass part. Then, with his right hand he added a running obbligato.

Together, Paderewski and the little boy thrilled the crowd. Success comes when we take the little we have and give it to God. He makes up the difference and says, "Don't quit — keep playing."

Remember to count the cost. If you don't, you may not have sufficient resources to finish what you start. Jesus said, *"Suppose one of you wants to build a tower. Will he not first sit down and estimate the cost to see if he has enough money to complete it? For if he lays the foundation and is not able to finish it, everyone who sees it will ridicule him saying, 'This fellow began to build and was not able to finish"* (Luke 14:28-30).

Having built two houses myself, I know firsthand

the wisdom of Jesus' words. If you have ever built a house you too know the necessity of counting the cost. About halfway through the process you ask yourself, "What in the world possessed me to do this?" The only sure way to finish construction on time and within budget is to count the cost.

So it is with any endeavor. Before launching a project, seeking a college degree, entering the ministry, starting a new business, changing careers, moving to another city, getting married or having children — count the cost. Make sure you have what it takes to finish what you start. It's all about determination.

Determination overcomes every obstacle and presses through every disappointment. Mother Theresa poignantly described determination in her poem, "Anyway."

People are often unreasonable, illogical and self-centered;
  Forgive them anyway.
If you are kind, people may accuse you of selfish, ulterior motives;
  Be kind anyway.
If you are successful, you will win some false friends and some true enemies;
  Succeed anyway.

*If you are honest and frank, people may cheat
you;*
  Be honest anyway.
*What you spend years building, someone could
destroy overnight;*
  Build anyway.
*If you find serenity and happiness, they may be
jealous;*
  Be happy anyway.
*The good you do today, people will often forget
tomorrow;*
  Do good anyway.
*Give the world the best you have, and it may never
be enough;*
  Give the world the best you have anyway.
*You see in the final analysis, it is between you and
God;*
  It was never between you and them anyway.

Linda Downs is the epitome of determination. In October of 1982, Linda became the first woman to complete the New York City marathon on crutches. She ran the 26.2 mile race on crutches because she was the victim of cerebral palsy.

She fell half a dozen times. Struggling to get back

up each time, she pressed toward the finish line. Eleven hours later she finished the race. She pushed through the pain to win the prize.

DEDICATION

"Come follow me," Jesus said,
"and I will make you fishers of men."
Matthew 4:19

You have to dedicate yourself to God, to the important people in your life and to your goals in order to succeed. To be dedicated means to commit oneself to a course of action. I know commitment is a lost word today. We prefer to talk about rights, needs, feelings and privileges. But there is no way to succeed without learning how to make and keep commitments.

Success comes mainly from hard work. There's no luck involved. William Temple, Archbishop of Canterbury said, "When I pray, coincidences happen, and when I do not, they don't."

Stephen Leacock said, "I am a great believer in luck and I find the harder I work, the more luck I have."

As a high school senior, I wrote a paper on the life

and work of American novelist William Faulkner. When asked what part inspiration played in his success he said, "My work is two-percent inspiration and 98 percent perspiration."

Barbie and I often tell our children, David Paul and Charlsi: *Your life is God's gift to you; what you do with your life is your gift to God.* God has endowed every person with gifts, talents and abilities, both naturally and spiritually. But God gives those gifts and abilities in their raw, undeveloped form. It's up to us to develop the gifts and then use them for His glory.

There's only one supreme task in life for us all: *To leave the world a little better off than when you arrived.* I mean, if you don't make the world a better place for others, there isn't much of a reason for being here, is there?

Jesus challenges us to do something significant with our lives. *"To whom much is given, much is required"* (Luke 12:48). We all fit into that category — *to whom much is given.* When you stop and think about it, we've all been given much. It's up to each one of us to take what we've been given and produce something with it.

There's an interesting story about Adam and Eve in the Bible. When God created Adam, He commissioned him to give names to all the animals. In fact, God *"brought them to the man to see what he would name them"* (Genesis 2:19). Man, not God, gave names to all the animals.

I find it fascinating that God watched to see what Adam would name them. I get the feeling that God still watches to see what each one of us will do with what He has given us.

I once read, *We are God-created, but self-molded.* God expects us to assume responsibility for our lives. So, as someone has aptly stated: *Control your thoughts — thoughts become words, words become actions, actions become habits, habits become character, character becomes destiny.*

Theodore Roosevelt said, "If you're not actively pursuing the person you want to be, then you're pursuing the person you don't want to be." When you clearly know the kind of person you want to be then dedicate yourself to becoming that person.

Dedication starts with **preparation**. Jesus said, *"Be dressed, ready for service"* (Luke 12:35). Being dressed means to be ready for action. Prepare yourself today for the opportunities you expect tomorrow. You see, when opportunity comes, it's time for action. At that point it's too late to get ready; you have to *be* ready when it comes. Otherwise, you will miss the opportunity. *Now* is the time to get ready.

We talk today about being dressed for success. If you go for a job interview you dress in such a way to help you get the job. When you go out on a date you dress for the occasion. Barbie and I just celebrated our 20th wedding anniversary. We met on a blind date. (The only one I ever had and look how it turned out — *Wonderful!*)

I still remember exactly what she was wearing on our first date. What she was wearing is none of your business, but let me assure you she got my attention. I proposed marriage, after knowing her for only eleven days. Talk about first impressions being lasting impressions!

Are you dressed and ready for opportunity? Many people get caught off guard by opportunity and miss it when it comes. Let me assure you — opportunity will come knocking at your door. And, contrary to popular opinion, opportunity will knock more than once. So, get ready! Whatever you prepare yourself for today will open the doors for you tomorrow.

Get ready for success!

Get ready for your dreams to come true!

Get ready for your prayers to be answered!

Get ready for your hard work to pay off!

Get ready...get ready...get ready!

You see, opportunity knocks on the door of preparation. Preparation attracts opportunities. Coach Joe Paterno, Penn. State University, says, "The will to win is important. The will to prepare is vital." You've got to give God something to bless.

Let me share a fascinating story with you about preparation found in the Old Testament.

The wife of a man from the company of the prophets cried out to Elisha, "Your servant my husband is dead, and you know that he revered the Lord. but now his creditor is coming to take my two boys as his slaves.

Elisha replied to her, "How can I help you? What do you have in your house?" "Your servant has nothing there at all," she said, "except a little oil." Elisha said, "Go around and ask all your neighbors for empty jars. Don't ask for just a few. Then go inside and shut the door behind you and your sons. Pour oil into all the jars, and as each is filled, put it to one side."

She left him and afterward shut the door behind her and her sons. They brought the jars to her and she kept pouring. When all the jars were full, she said to her son, "Bring me another one." But he replied, "There is not a jar left." Then the oil stopped flowing.

She went and told the man of God, and he said, "Go, sell the oil and pay your debts. You and your sons can live on what is left." (2 Kings 4:1-7)

She needed a miracle. She needed financial provisions to meet her debt obligation. She needed the blessing of God and she asked for it. But the blessing only came when she made preparation. She had to give God something to bless. For her, it meant collecting all the jars she could. She gave God jars to bless.

I like what Elisha told her, "Don't ask for just a few jars." In other words, raise your level of expectation. Your level of preparation will determine your level of success. If you offer God a few jars, you'll get a small blessing. But if you bring Him as many jars as you can find, like she did, you'll receive *"immeasurably more than you ask or even think"* (Ephesians 3:20). God still fills up jars of preparation with abundant blessings.

His question to her is crucial in the equation of success: "What do you have in your house?" I ask you the same question, What do you have that you can give God to bless? Give Him your time, talents, abilities, education, ideas, creativity — everything you have. That's how you prepare yourself for opportunity.

Barbie and I started our first church in Athens, Georgia. We were only 25 at the time. We started with 12 members and a small building. Our first Sunday was a big day, as you can imagine. We only had one family with children and Barbie was our first children's minister. The problem was the only family with kids had gone to Florida for the weekend.

During Sunday School, I went to the children's classroom to see Barbie. The room was well prepared. She had an exciting program planned. But no kids. I'll never forget the look of disappointment on her face when I walked into that empty room. "I don't have any children to teach today," she said sadly.

I replied, "Well, let's do something about it. Let's take ten chairs, put them in a circle and envision them filled with children." So we did. Then we joined our hands and prayed that God would fill those chairs. And He did. Many times over. After ten years we had several hundred children and young people in church every Sunday.

By putting out those chairs we were preparing ourselves for opportunity. We gave God something to bless. So, give God something to bless. Then stand back and watch Him work.

Second, dedication requires **motivation**. To motivate means to incite to action, to stir with passion and to impel forward. Let me share something very important with you — You are responsible for your motivation. Sure, it's great when family and friends encourage you, but you can't depend totally on them. You have to keep yourself motivated.

Everyone has goals. But only people who can motivate themselves through tough times reach their goals. The old adage says, "The road to hell is paved with good intentions."

Surround yourself with positive people. Negative people will pull you down and rob you of your dreams. You need positive people who will lift you up and make you believe in yourself.

Ask God to give you new motivation if you feel burned out. I have discovered prayer to be an incredibly inspiring and motivating experience. When I pray my thoughts are clearer, my attitude is more positive, my outlook is more hopeful, my concern for others is deeper, and my resolve to press on toward my goals is stronger.

Maintaining motivation also requires keeping focus. Keep your eye on the finish line to win the prize. Fight off every distraction that diverts your attention away from your goals.

A man driving through the Midwest came to a rundown gas station and grocery store in the middle of nowhere. The sign read: *Last stop for gas for 100 miles.*

He stopped at the station and filled up his car.

He went in to pay. The owner was a rough, rugged old-timer. As the man paid the owner, he noticed a big pot of black coffee brewing behind the counter. The sign read: *World Famous Chicory Coffee.*

He turned to leave when the old-timer said, "Wait. Won't you try a cup of my world famous chicory coffee?"

"Thanks, but not today," replied the traveler.

"Come on, try a cup."

"No, thank you."

At that the old-timer pulled out a gun, pointed it at the man and demanded, "I said drink a cup of my world famous chicory coffee!"

Trembling, he took a cup and started to drink it down. He nearly choked on the coffee.

When he finished, the old-timer handed him the gun and said, "Now, hold the gun on me while I drink a cup!"

The point of the story is don't wait until someone holds a gun on you before you get motivated to succeed. Keep yourself fired up! *"Fan into flame the gift of God that is in you"* (2 Timothy 1:7).

Dedication requires preparation, motivation and, finally, **action**. Don't be a talker, be a doer. Success follows action. I read somewhere that there are three kinds of business people: successful, unsuccessful and those giving seminars telling the second group how the first group did it.

When we take family vacations we experience some tension in the planning process. Barbie likes to see things when we travel. So, she plans site-seeing ventures. But I tell her that the kids and I don't go on vacation to see things, we go to *do* things.

One year we took a family vacation to Arizona. We were driving outside Phoenix. The mountains were majestic. Barbie commented on how beautiful the mountains were. So I impulsively stopped the car, pulled over to the side of the road and announced, "Let's go climb that mountain!"

She said, "You've got to be kidding. We can't do that." The kids joined in with me. "Yeah, Dad, let's go climb it!" We coerced her into coming with us, took all the bottled water we had and spent a couple of hours climbing this small mountain. We ran out of water, got in a couple of tight places and had to help to each other make the climb.

We found ourselves in a precarious situation near the nest of two large eagles with massive claws. But we had a great time. I mean, the kids and I had a great time. (I couldn't get her to climb any more mountains the rest of the trip.)

My point is, don't spend your life driving down the interstate of life looking at all the magnificent scenes. Get in the action and do something with what God has given you! Live life. Don't settle for watching others live it.

There are three reasons why we don't take action. First, we get caught in the trap of *the paralysis of analysis*. We spend so much time analyzing situations and opportunities that we fail to act.

Secondly, we procrastinate because *we're afraid of failure*. But the only people who never fail are those who never try anything. If you try, you will fail. That's okay. Rebounding from failure is fundamental to success. I have made two important resolutions recently.

Resolution #1: *I promise to make my fair share of mistakes.*

Resolution #2: *I promise to keep on trying until I reach my goals.*

Mark Twain said, "Twenty years from now you will be more disappointed by the things you didn't do than by the ones you did do. So throw off the bowlines. Sail away from the safe harbor. Catch the trade winds in your sails. Explore. Dream. Discover."

Finally, we avoid taking action because *we aim for perfection*. God doesn't expect us to be perfect, He only asks us to be faithful. *Life is not a spelling bee!*, as Harold Kushner says.

When you make one mistake in a spelling bee you're out of the game. It's all or nothing. Life is more like a baseball season — long and drawn out. You don't have to win all the games to have a winning season. Just win a few more games than you lose, and you'll have a winning season. So it is with life.

Dedication requires us to take full advantage of every opportunity that comes our way. It's easy to miss opportunities. Don't take them for granted. Some opportunities don't come around very often. So, when opportunity comes, make the most of it.

According to legend, a man was walking one night in the desert. Suddenly, a voice said to him, "Pick up a handful of pebbles and put them in your pocket, and tomorrow you will be both sorry and glad."

The man obeyed. He stooped down, picked up a handful of pebbles and put them in his pocket. The next morning he reached into his pocket and found diamonds and rubies and emeralds. He was both glad and sorrowful. Glad that he had taken some pebbles yet sorry he hadn't taken more. So it is with opportunity.

Remember, your life is God's gift to you. What you do with your life is your gift back to God. So, do something great for God with your life.

In May 1792, a most significant event transpired in Nottingham, England. William Carey stood before a group of ministers and delivered what has been called the greatest missionary sermon in church history. At that time there were no missionary societies anywhere in the world.

William Carey made a map of the world, placed it on the wall of his cobbler shop and began to pray for the whole world. He became so concerned for the people of India that he left home and went to Bengal, India. He preached there for seven years before he had his first convert. Carey said, "Expect great things from God; attempt great things for God."

Take a few minutes and reflect on these questions concerning dedication.

✔ *What are you doing with your life today to give it back to God as a gift?*

✔ *Are you preparing yourself spiritually, mentally, physically, financially, and relationally to meet the next opportunity?*

✔ *Are you fully motivated in every area of your life? Or, have you lost your zeal and enthusiasm? Do you need to fan into flame the gift of God that is in you?*

✔ *Are you sitting on the sideline instead of playing in the game of life? Now is the time to take action!*

DEPENDABILITY

*"Now it is required that those who have been
given a trust must prove faithful."*
1 Corinthians 4:2

Thousands of fans in Camden Yards baseball stadium stood to their feet September 6, 1995 to honor one man, Cal Ripken, Jr. Exuberant fans cheered for twenty minutes, stopping the game to salute the Baltimore Orioles shortstop.

Why? Other players had better statistics. Five other Orioles held higher batting averages that year; three hit more home runs. The fans cheered Cal because he set the new record for most consecutive games played: 2,131. They cheered his faithfulness. He was dependable. They knew they could count on Cal.

Did you know that people are counting on you? You need to succeed not only for yourself, but also for those who are depending on you.

"That's a lot of pressure," you may be thinking.

Sure it is, but we need the pressure of dependability in order to succeed. That's what keeps us going. If people weren't counting on us we wouldn't reach our potential.

Take a minute and reflect on the people who are counting on you. Write their names on a list. There are probably more persons than you realize. Begin everyday by telling yourself, *"Today, God, my family and my friends are counting on me. And I'm not going to let them down."*

No one succeeds alone. So, identify the key persons in your life. Who are your role models? Who are you accountable to? Who are key leaders in your life? Who are the people who are dependent on you? Who are your close friends who are committed to helping you reach your goals?

Dependability starts with the little things in life. A popular book says, Don't sweat the small stuff. But there is some small stuff you need to sweat if you expect to get ahead in life. Jesus taught this basic law of success: *"You have been faithful with a few things; I will put you in charge of many things."* (Matthew 25:23).

Here's the best way to get promoted: Be dependable with the few things you have been given, and you will be rewarded with greater position and prosperity.

Some people feel they are too good to do certain jobs; like it's beneath their dignity to perform simple tasks. They're the ones who like to pray, "Lord, use me, especially in a supervisory capacity." But you can't supervise until you're willing to get your hands dirty.

Every successful person starts at the bottom and works his or her way to the top. It is that very process that prepares a person to lead. Without it, their leadership lacks compassion, humility and a servant's heart.

True leaders have paid their dues. They've earned their success. No one handed it to them on a silver platter. They're well aquatinted with hard work. As a result, they show sensitivity and understanding to the people they lead.

I have a close friend who has built a very successful business. His oldest son has the opportunity to take a leadership role in the company in the future. His father has taught him the business. How? By starting him at the bottom, putting him to work in the field, and learning the business from the ground up.

Now he's in college studying business management. He'll be fully prepared for success because he's earning it the proper way. When he leads others, he will do it from the perspective of having been there and done it himself. And people listen to the wisdom of personal experience.

During the American Revolutionary War, a man on horseback came across a squad of soldier's trying to move a heavy tree which had fallen across a road. The corporal stood by giving orders. "Heave!" But the timber was too heavy.

"Why don't you help them?" the man asked.

"Who, me? I'm a corporal."   .

So, the man dismounted and took his place with the soldiers. "All together now," he said. "Heave!" Together they lifted the heavy timber.

The stranger mounted his horse and told the corporal, "The next time you have a piece of timber for your men to handle, send for the commander-in-chief." The stranger was George Washington.

So, be dependable with what you have today and God will reward you with greater blessings tomorrow. In fact, it's amazing what you can produce with just a little. After all, Jesus only needed five loaves and two fish to feed a multitude. And He said you could move a mountain with just a mustard seed of faith.

Great things have been accomplished by people who were faithful with the little they had. After 23 years with the IRS Anne Sheiber, retired from her job in 1944. During her years of service, she had never earned more than $4,000 a year and never received a promotion, despite having a law degree and leading her office in turning up underpayments and underreporting.

When she retired she took her savings of $5,000 and invested it in the stock market. Some fifty years later, in January 1995, Anne died at the young age of 101. By that time her $5,000 investment had grown to $22 million in stocks. She made all her investment decisions, reviewing *The Wall Street Journal* daily, and her portfolio included such blue chip stocks as Coca-Cola and Paramount Studios. She willed all her stock holdings to Yeshiva University in New York — a university that had never even heard of her.

You don't need *more* to be successful — more talent, more money, more opportunity, more faith, more confidence — you just need to use what you have. Be faithful with a few things. Then you will be promoted to do greater things!

Make sure your dream in life is big enough to keep you motivated. Victor Frankl, who survived Hitler's death camps, pondered the plight of those who have enough to live on but not enough to live for. God says, *"Call to me and I will answer you and tell you great and unsearchable things, things you do not know"* (Jeremiah 33:3).

When Apple Computer fell on difficult times, Apple's young chairman Steve Jobs, traveled from Silicon Valley to New York City. His purpose was to convince PepsiCo's John Sculley to move west and revitalize the struggling company.

As the two men overlooked the Manhattan skyline from Sculley's penthouse office, the Pepsi executive started to decline Jobs's offer. "Financially," Sculley said, "you'd have to give me a million-dollar salary, a million-dollar bonus and a million-dollar severance."

Stunned, Jobs agreed, that is, if Sculley would move to California. But Sculley would only commit to being a consultant from New York. At that Steve issued him a challenge — "Do you want to spend the rest of your life selling sugared water, or do you want to change the world?"

In his autobiography *Odyssey*, Sculley admits Jobs's challenge "knocked the wind out of me." He said that he had become so caught up in his comfort zone that an opportunity to change the world nearly passed him by. Instead, he reevaluated his life and went to Apple.[1]

You need to commit yourself to a cause greater than yourself. Set goals that will stretch you beyond your comfort zone. Are you being stretched in your career, education, or life right now? The only way to step up to the next level is to be challenged. You need an environment which challenges you to move upward and onward in life.

Jesus gave His followers such a challenge: *"Go into all the world and make disciples of all nations"* (Matthew 28:19). Now, that was a tall order for that ragtag group He called His apostles. But they had learned to trust Him. They had learned to dream big. And if Jesus believed they could do it, then they believed it too. Before the end of the first century they had carried the good news of Jesus and His love to the known world of that time. He taught them to dream big and to live for a cause greater than themselves.

Do you have such a cause in your life that fills each day with purpose? If you do, it will bring out the best in you. You too will rise to meet the challenge.

As a young man, John C. Rockefeller, Sr. demonstrated strength and determination in his goals. By age 33, he earned his first million dollars. By age 43, he controlled the largest company in the world. At age 53, he was the richest man in the world and the world's only billionaire.

He then contracted a rare disease. His hair fell out,

his eyebrows and eyelashes disappeared, and he was shrunken like a mummy. While his weekly income was one million dollars, his diet consisted of milk and crackers. He was so anxious that he maintained bodyguards. Unable even to sleep, he lost all joy for living.

The medical doctors predicted he would not live another year. The newspaper wrote his obituary in advance. During those sleepless nights he began to take stock of himself. He realized that he could not take any of his money with him into the next world.

He made a new resolution. He began giving his money to hospitals, medical research and missions work. He helped the poor and needy. He established the Rockefeller Foundation whose funding led to the discovery of penicillin as well as cures for malaria, tuberculosis, and diphtheria.

He began to sleep again. The symptoms began to disappear. He became happy again. Instead of dying at 54 as predicted, he lived to be 98. He was faithful with what God gave him.

I was privileged to hear Mother Teresa speak at the National Prayer Breakfast in Washington, D.C., in 1994. She was a woman dedicated to a cause greater than herself. She was faithful to what God called her to do. Thousands of orphaned children in India and families living in poverty depended on the ministry and care of Mother Teresa. They knew they could count on her.

She once said, "I know God will not give me anything I can't handle. I just wish that He didn't trust me so much."

My mentor in the ministry, Dr. Paul Walker, is a man of faithfulness. He has been the single greatest influence on my ministry. As a teenager, I had the privilege of spending many hours in the Walkers' home, being a close friend of their late and oldest son, Paul Dana. I also watched carefully Dr. Walker's leadership of the church. For 37 years, he and his wife Carmelita, pastored the congregation in Atlanta, which my wife and I now have the privilege to pastor.

Of all the things I learned from him about life and ministry, the most important is to be faithful in what God has called you to do. His long tenure is a testimony to his "stickability," if I can coin a term.

You have to learn to stick with your plan and to persevere through every challenge until you cross the finish line. Dedication means to *"run with perseverance the race marked out for us"* (Hebrews 12:1).

Success belongs only to those who are faithful in what God calls them to do. People are counting on you, and so is God. So, do your part faithfully. Not perfectly, I might add, but faithfully.

DEVELOPMENT

"The path of the righteous is like the first gleam of dawn,
shining ever brighter till the full light of day."
Proverbs 4:18

A group of tourists were visiting a beautiful village. They passed by an old man sitting beside a fence. In a patronizing way one tourist asked him, "Were any great men born in this village?"

"No," the man replied. "Only babies."

There are no instant heroes, or champions or even saints. Growth takes time. It's progression not perfection that counts in life. At times, success is simply taking three steps forward, and two steps back.

There are two basic laws of life in conflict with each other: the law of development versus the law of deterioration. Whatever fails to grow, dies. To grow means, "to increase in size, amount and degree; to come to be gradually; and to progress toward maturity." Are you growing and developing? Or, are you drifting with the tide, settling for status quo?

You can't stand still and expect to succeed. The status quo is the prelude to deterioration for any organization or any relationship. We either develop or we deteriorate. We either advance or we retreat.

The watchwords of success are *press on!* Regardless of your fears, your failures, your frustrations, your problems, your disappointments, or your struggles, press on to win the prize!

This is not to say that success requires a driven lifestyle where we're constantly pushing ahead without times to rest. Far from it. Progress includes plateaus. Geographically, the word *plateau* means an extensive stretch of elevated level land. Psychologically, the word refers to a stable interval in the progress of a person's learning ability. Financially, the term denotes stability in economy reflecting neither gains nor losses. Generally, the word describes any stage in the leveling off in the development of something.

Nothing can continue its long-term pattern of growth without seasons of plateaus. The plateau experience enables us to assimilate previous learning so we can go on to the next level. The problem occurs when we linger at the plateau too long. When this occurs, the plateau experience turns to stagnation and stagnation then leads to deterioration.

Life is not a sprint, its a marathon. You need a marathon mentality to succeed. So, settle in for the long-haul. Pace yourself. And by all means, keep making progress and you will reach your goals.

Let me share with you eight important principles about how we develop.

First, **growth is personal**. No two people grow just alike. Parents know this truth all too well. As a father, I have to deal with my two children very differently. Their personalities are unique and require special attention.

For example, if Barbie and I want information from our son David Paul, we have to have him interrogated by the FBI. Charlsi, on the other hand, is an open book. She will tell you everything she knows.

When she was about six years old she overheard Barble and I disagreeing about something one Saturday night. The next morning at Sunday School, when the teacher took prayer requests, Charlsi blurted out, "Ya'll pray for my parents. They're having marriage problems." Talk about being embarrassed by your kids.

Barbie and I are very different. Sure, we share some things in common but our personalities are different on many points. She, for example, is highly structured. I'm more spontaneous. Our first vacations use to be tough. She wanted to plan every detail and I wanted to play it by ear. Over the years we've learned to balance each other out. She's more spontaneous now and I'm more structured.

The point is be who you are. Don't compare your progress with others. Just focus on your own development and progress. Don't try to be somebody else. Be the best *you*, you can be.

Growth is progressive. Growth takes time. I once read, "The conversion of a soul is the miracle of a moment but the manufacturing of a saint takes a lifetime." We live in the fast lane. We want something, and we want it now! We have microwave ovens, PCs, PDAs, pocket calculators, credit cards, fast-food restaurants (an oxymoron by the way), diet-pills, fax machines, disposable diapers and every imaginable convenience to make life easier and faster.

But you can't rush maturity. It takes time…

for character to develop,

to learn new skills,

to get an education,

to master a musical instrument, and

to learn a sport. (Except for golf, which you will never learn!)

Personal growth and patience travel hand in hand.

So, look out for the trap of perfectionism. The perfectionist says...

I have to be perfect to be worthwhile.

I have to please everybody.

I must do everything right for God to love me.

I must do everything perfectly or not at all.

These four inner beliefs keep perfectionists depressed and defeated. Remember, you can't have all ups. Life also has downs. It takes time to reach your goals.

Growth is pleasurable. We feel better about ourselves when we make progress in any area of life. We conquer a bad habit. We gain control over a judgmental attitude. We become more compassionate. We reach our goals. We become better managers of money. We get a promotion we've worked for. We learn to communicate better at home. The joyful person can say, "I'm not the person I want to be, but praise God, I'm not the person I used to be."

Success requires excellence. *"Whatever you do, work at it with all your heart"* (Colossians 3:23). Barbie and I have the opportunity to speak at leadership conferences, usually for ministers. We always encourage them that if they want to find fulfillment in their work focus on *quality* not *quantity*.

I've learned that quantity follows quality. A leader can't always control the quantity of his or her work — how much money is earned, how many customers frequent a business or how many parishioners attend church — but they can always control the quality of their work and product. If you want to succeed, don't strive to be the biggest, strive to be the best!

Being the best you can be, and providing the best product and service you can, will generate bigger results. Quality is a goal every person and organization can reach. You can be the best *you* can be. You aren't really competing with anyone else in the race of success. You only compete against yourself.

The story is told of a stonecutter in the Middle Ages who was working on a Gothic cathedral. He had spent days and weeks hewing out the features of a small figure to be placed on the top of the cathedral — not one of the prominent gargoyles that would sit atop the corners of the roof, but a smaller statue, which would be tucked away in an obscure nook.

An onlooker, who had been watching these painstaking efforts, came up to the sculptor and said: "That's going to be a beautiful statue, but tell me, Why are you working so hard on it when you know that no one will see it when you put it in its place?"

The stonecutter replied, "God will see it."

That's excellence. A great sense of personal pride comes from knowing you have done your best even though others may not see it.

Growth is painful. It's true — *No pain, no gain.* Everyone who is committed to a nutrition program or an exercise program knows firsthand the reality of that adage. People who grind it out through college, graduate school, business training and other educational and career enhancing opportunities, know the truth of, *No pain, no gain.* There's a price to pay for success.

A man found a cocoon of the emperor moth and took it home to watch it emerge. One day a small opening appeared and for several hours the moth struggled to get out but couldn't seem to push its body past a certain point.

The man decided something was wrong. So, he took a pair of scissors and cut an opening in the cocoon allowing the moth to emerge easily. But its body was swollen and the wings were small and shriveled.

He thought that in a few hours the wings would spread out in their amazing beauty, but they didn't. Instead of flying freely the moth dragged its swollen body and shriveled wings around.

The struggle necessary for the moth to pass through

the cocoon is God's way of forcing fluid from the body into the wings for their full development. The man's intervention to help did nothing but maim the moth.

Sometimes the struggle is exactly what we need to help us grow and reach our potential. That's exactly why we need to stay off the path of least resistance we discussed earlier. Instead, take a route that will make you become the best person you can be.

Growth is productive. Personal growth results in productivity. God put us here on earth to produce something with our lives and to give something back to the world. Erma Bombeck said, "When I stand before God at the end of my life, I would hope that I would not have a single bit of talent left but could say, 'I used everything you gave me.'"

One of my closest friends is many years my senior. His name is Arvel Burell. He worked for the Gulf Oil Corporation for 37 years and then retired. Then, he took a position as business administrator for the church, where I serve as pastor. He is still holding that position after 22 years of service! Now, he is the epitome of productivity. The reason he continues to work is because he believes he is doing what God has called him to do.

The problem with many people is that they approach opportunities by asking, what's in it for me? Instead of asking, what contribution can I make to benefit others? Always taking — seldom giving.

There are two kinds of people in the world — those who take out more than they put in, and those who put in more than they take out.

Take economics, for example. Financial security and wealth is based on one basic principle: You have to put more money into your investments than you take out. If not, you will simply run out of resources.

It's a simple law of life. Did you know that the average American family today spends 115 percent of their net annual income? They live under constant financial pressure for one reason — they take out more than they put in.

Or, consider relationships. People can take out more from a relationship than they put in. This happens to a lot of marriages. Couples place constant demands on each other until nothing is left. They drain their relationship dry. Only when you put something into your relationships, will you be able to draw out what you need. So, if you don't like what you're getting from your relationships stop and consider what you're putting in.

Growth is proactive. Where you are going is more

important than where you've been. Life is ahead of you, not behind you. So don't waste time and energy reacting to problems and pressures. Success is not measured by solving problems; it is measured by reaching goals.

Each day is a new day. Forget the things which are behind. Let yesterday be yesterday. Today offers a new set of challenges and opportunities. It is impossible to grow and reach your potential as long as you hold on to the pains and problems of the past.

A farmer had an apple tree that had been blown over by the wind and uprooted. A passerby asked him, "What are you going to do with the tree?"

The farmer replied, "I am going to gather the fruit and then burn the tree." So, it is with the past, especially with failures and disappointments. Gather the fruit. Learn what you can. Then burn the tree — put the past behind you and move on.

A man I once worked with told me, "Never bring me a problem without a proposed solution." I maintain that same standard with my staff. No one is ready to solve a problem until they have explored every possible solution. Focusing on problems is reactive. Focusing on solutions is proactive.

Too many people get stuck in life wondering *why*

something has happened to them instead of focusing on *what* they can do about it. Keep your focus on solving problems (or seizing opportunities). Keep your life moving in a forward direction.

Growth is a partnership. There are no self-made success stories. Successful people have a lot of help in achieving success. Always give credit and thanks to your parents, your teachers, your mentors, your friends and your associates for your accomplishments. True success is a team effort. And remember to give God all the glory. He's the best partner you have.

Vince Lombardi put teamwork into perspective: "The challenge for every organization is to build a feeling of oneness, of dependence on one another...because the question is usually not how well each person works but how well they work together."

An airplane is a good example of teamwork. I once read that an airplane can be defined as "millions of parts flying together in close formation."

For me, teamwork means that I don't recruit people to work *for* me, I recruit them to work *with* me. Working for someone is demeaning; working with someone is dynamic. When Jesus selected the Twelve, He chose them *"that they might be with Him"* (Mark 3:15). Note their relationship was *with* Him not *for* Him.

Late in the 15th century, two young apprentice wood carvers in France wanted to study painting. But such study would take money and both Hans and Albrecht were poor. They decided that one would work and earn income while the other studied. Then, when the educated one became successful he would help the other. They tossed a coin and Albrecht won.

While Albrecht studied in Venice, Hans worked as a blacksmith. As he earned money he sent it to his friend. The months stretched into years. At last Albrecht returned home a master painter.

Now it was his turn to help Hans. When they met together, Albrecht couldn't help but notice Hans' hands. They were callused and bruised from the many years of heavy labor in the blacksmith shop. His fingers could never handle a delicate painter's brush. Albrecht was touched by the sacrifice of his friend.

In humble gratitude to Hans for his years of sacrifice, the artist, the great Albrecht Durer, painted a portrait of the work-worn hands that had labored so faithfully so that he might develop his talent. He presented this painting of praying hands to his devoted friend. Since then, the famous praying hands have been seen by millions.

Finally, **growth is positive**. We talk about growing

up, not growing *down.* Growing up sounds positive. Everybody wants to move up in life and climb the ladder of success. Who ever got excited about corporate *downsizing?* We'd rather have corporate *up-sizing!* You see, the whole idea of growth is positive.

Whenever a staff member comes to me with a "problem," I say, "You mean an opportunity, don't you?"

Reluctantly, they concede, "Yes, I mean an opportunity."

Success requires that we turn every problem into an opportunity for personal growth or the advancement of our goals.

I refuse to listen to people talk about their problems. That's too negative. When we turn problems into opportunities, and see them in a positive light, then we are poised to do something about them. I've said that so often to my staff that they'll correct themselves in midstream — "We have a problem...I mean an *opportunity.*"

The only person it doesn't work too well with is my wife. When Barbie says, "We have a problem," and I respond, "You mean an opportunity."

She says, "No, I mean a *problem!*"

If you like boating, fishing or water skiing, you're familiar with the name *Evinrude.* Ole Evinrude was in love and engaged to be married. He and his fiancé went out on a beautiful summer's day to row across the lake and enjoy a picnic on the other side. Just as they finished setting up the picnic, she realized that they had forgotten the dessert.

So, Ole rowed the boat back across the lake. He picked up the dessert and started making the lengthy row back across. About halfway, he was exhausted. The heat and the rowing had nearly drained him. While the ice cream melted he thought, "There's got to be a better way."

That exasperated thought prompted him to invent the first portable outboard motor. Ole's experimentation began in 1906. By 1909, he had produced the first commercially successful outboard motor. In 1910, he was granted a patent for his invention. His company went on to dominate the market for years. He turned an obstacle into an opportunity.

Successful people generate positive power. They can transform a family, a church, an organization or a corporation by their contagious spirit of faith. Think about it. All the truly successful people you know are positive people. They have what we might call a "yes face."

During his presidency, Thomas Jefferson and a group

of companions were traveling on horseback. They came to a swollen river, overflowing its banks. Each rider risked his life as he crossed on horseback fighting the rapid currents.

After several crossed successfully, a stranger asked the President if he would ferry him across the river. Without hesitation, Jefferson agreed. The stranger mounted Jefferson's horse and together they crossed the river.

Once across the river, the stranger dismounted his horse. Someone asked him, "Tell me, why did you ask the President to ferry you across?"

The man was shocked, not knowing it was the President who had taken him across. Then he said, "All I know is that on some of your faces was written the answer No, and on others the answer, Yes. His was a Yes face."

Now, let's review the seven spiritual laws of success:

1. **Direction:** *Know where you're going and how you plan to get there.*

2. **Desire:** *Possess a strong sense of passion about life and what you want to achieve.*

3. **Discipline:** *Control your thoughts, feelings, and actions.*

4. **Determination:** *Press on toward your goals in spite of every obstacle you face.*

5. **Dedication:** *Commit yourself to God, the important people in your life, and your goals.*

6. **Dependability:** *Be faithful with what you have. Remember, we're counting on you.*

7. **Development:** *Keep making progress and move forward with your life. Turn your problems into opportunities and take advantage of them.*

I want leave you with a story that has greatly impacted the way I see success. A beggar sat everyday on a street corner across from an artist's studio. Day after the day, the artist saw him and decided to paint his portrait.

After a couple of days, he finished the portrait. Then he walked across the street to the beggar and invited him to his studio. "There's something I want you to see," he told him. Once inside the studio, the artist unveiled the portrait.

At first the beggar didn't recognize himself. "Who is it?" he kept asking. The artist just smiled and said nothing.

Then suddenly the man saw himself in the portrait. Not as he was, in his dejected state, but as he could be.

"Is that me? Is it really me?," he asked excitedly.

"That's the man I see in you," the artist replied.

The beggar said, "If that's the man you see then that's the man I'll be."